NARROW GAUGE INSPIRATION

PETER SMITH

Copyright © 2013 Peter Smith

All rights reserved.

ISBN-10: 149359009X

ISBN-13: 978149 3590094

CHAPTERS

1. INTRODUCTION — Page 1
2. St LAURENT du PONT — Page 2
3. FOURVOIRIE — Page 7
4. PONT de VAUX 1 — Page 12
5. PONT de VAUX 2 — Page 18
6. CHATEAUNEUF 1 — Page 21
7. CHATEAUNEUF 2 — Page 27
8. BREZOLLES — Page 32
9. St JAMES — Page 39
10. TIGY — Page 46
11. VALLEE DE CELLES — Page 53
12. St. ROMAIN — Page 61

CHAPTER 1
INTRODUCTION

Imagine the scene; a meeting of the town council in a small provincial town in England. A local business man has proposed building a narrow gauge railway along the High Street, across the middle of the market place, in front of the town hall to terminate at a station squeezed between Woolworths and WH Smiths (or whatever the Victorian equivalent was).

It wouldn't have stood a chance, would it!

In France, it not only happened, it was positively encouraged. A town without a railway or tramway couldn't hold its head up high, it wasn't really fit to call itself a town at all. It would have averted its gaze, ashamed to be in the company of real towns that did have a railway running along the High Street!

This of course was a delight to the enthusiast, although slightly less so to those unfortunate enough to have invested money is such concerns. Not many survived to see out the 1930's.

With so many little lines to choose from there is a cornucopia of wonderful scenes to inspire the modeller; this book presents a selection that I find irresistible. I hope you enjoy than as much as I do.

CHAPTER 2
St LAURENT du PONT

I had to begin with this, possibly the oddest narrow gauge station in France and one which cries out to be modelled……believe it or not it was deliberately built like this, it wasn't a conversion job.

You remember the old song 'The railroad runs through the middle of the house'? Well, here it really did!

The 35km long line ran between Voiron and Saint Beron in the Isere and Savoie regions and was metre gauge. It opened in 1895 and ran until 1936. The branch line to Fourvoirie Chartreuse distillery passed under the porch of the building, with the main Voiron Saint-Beron line in the foreground.

The station here housed the Hotel de la Gare on the first floor, which must have been interesting for the guests. The usual booking office and so on were on the ground floor.

So, not only do you have this wonderful station, but the trains were running to a distillery…what more could you want?

St-LAURENT-du-PONT. - Avenue de la Grande-Chartreuse

Here's the best part – the building is still there. Looking at it now you would have no idea about its past use, it looks pretty conventional, but when you compare it with the old postcards it all becomes clear. It hasn't actually changed much at all.

CHEMIN DE FER DE VOIRON A SAINT-BÉRON

(1re, 2e classes.)

CORRESPONDANCES POUR LA GRANDE-CHARTREUSE

(1) Halte ouverte au service des voyageurs sans bagages.

fr. c.	fr. c.	kil. De Voiron							
» 30	» 15	3	●Voiron (102, 199) dép.	...	7 12	9 45	12 40	16 25	19 50
» 35	» 25	4	La Buisse (1)	...	7 19	9 53	12 48	16 34	19 58
» 55	» 35	6	Coublevie	...	7 24	9 58	12 53	16 40	20 3
» 75	» 45	8	Croix-Bayard (1)	...	7 29	10 3	12 59	16 46	20 8
1 10	» 70	12	St-Étienne-d-Crossey	...	7 38	10 12	13 8	16 55	20 17
1 30	» 80	14	Pont-de-Demay (1)	...	7 52	10 26	13 22	17 11	20 32
1 65	1 »	18	St-Joseph-de-Rivière	...	7 57	10 32	13 28	17 17	20 38
1 65	1 »	18	Le Cotterg (1)	...	8 8	10 38	13 34	17 24	20 44
1 65	1 »	18	St-Laurent-d-P.(Ville)	...	8 8	10 43	13 39	17 30	20 50
			St-Laurent-du-]arr.		8 10	10 45	13 41	17 32	20 52
			Pont (Revol)...]dép.	5 46	8 18	10 55	13 49	17 50	20 56
2 05	1 25	22	Aiguenoire (1)	5 54	8 25	11 3	13 56	17 58	21 4
2 20	1 35	24	Entre-Deux-Guiers	6 2	8 32	11 11	14 4	18 10	21 10
2 40	1 45	24	Les Echelles	6 10	8 35	11 ─	14 6	18 20	...
2 60	1 60	27	La Croix-d-l-Roche(1)	6 16	8 41	...	14 12	18 26	...
2 80	1 60	28	Chailles	6 20	8 45	...	14 18	18 30	...
3 15	1 95	34	●St-Béron (97, 197) arr.	6 40	9 5	...	14 38	18 50	...

fr. c.	fr. c.	kil. De St-Béron							
» 55	» 35	6	●St-Béron......dép.	...	7 22	9 37	...	16 40	19 44
» 95	» 55	9	Chailles	...	7 41	9 57	...	17 1	20 4
1 15	» 95	10	La Croix-d-l-Roche(1)	...	7 45	10 1	13 30	17 5	20 8
1 25	» 55	10	Les Echelles	...	7 52	10 12	13 36	17 15	20 16
1 45	» 75	13	Entre-Deux-Guiers	5 14	7 55	10 22	13 44	17 26	20 22
1 50	» 90	16	Aiguenoire (1)	5 20	8 —	10 28	13 44	17 32	20 28
			St-Laurent-du-]arr.	5 28	8 8	10 36	13 57	17 40	20 35
			Pont (Revol)...]dép.	5 38	8 14	10 46	14 4	18 —	...
1 50	» 90	16	St-Laurent-d-P.(Ville)	5 41	8 17	10 49	14 7	18 3	...
1 85	1 15	20	Le Cotterg (1)	5 45	8 21	10 53	14 11	18 7	...
2 05	1 25	22	St-Joseph-de-Rivière	5 52	8 28	11 —	14 16	18 14	...
2 40	1 45	26	Pont-de-Demay (1)	5 58	8 33	11 5	14 21	18 20	...
2 60	1 60	28	St-Étienne-d-Crossey	6 13	8 48	11 21	14 32	18 36	...
2 80	1 70	30	Croix-Bayard (1)	6 21	8 56	11 29	14 40	18 44	...
2 85	1 75	31	Coublevie	6 27	9 —	11 —	14 46	18 50	...
3 »	1 85	31	La Buisse (1)	6 32	9 5	11 30	14 50	18 54	...
3 15	1 95	34	●Voiron......arr.	6 40	9 12	11 47	14 58	19 2	...

CHAPTER 3

FOURVOIRIE

But what about the distillery? Funny stations are all very well, but a distillery, now that's a real destination for a railway!

The Chartreuse distillery at Fourvoirie was run by Carthusian monks and the short branch line was opened in 1895 to a station, and then right into the distillery itself.

This is the station, delightful in its own right with the covered roof over the loading platform on the left, with the goods shed proper beyond it.

The station is on the left, with the distillery beyond. On a model they could be brought a lot closer, of course.

Here's the line into the distillery, with Pinguely 030 tank shunting box vans, presumably to be loaded with barrels.

The distillery was a big place; the railway came in at the far end and ran along the valley in the background. In the lower picture you can just see the rails along the left of the road running towards the gate.

The line closed to passengers together with the main route in 1931; freight carried on until 1936 when the railway was closed down.

The distillery is still there of course, and happily so is the station, beautifully restored as a private house.

CHAPTER 4
PONT de VAUX PART 1

In the introduction I imagined a line crossing the town market place; here's the classic example of just that, and not one but two lines. The town is Pont de Vaux.

Pont-de-Vaux was very busy at the intersection of two metre gauge lines of the Tramways de l'Ain. The two trains are on the line connecting Saint-Trivier-de-Courtes to Trévoux which opened in 1897, the other line being to Fleurville which opened as an independent company in 1900. Both routes closed in 1936.

Normally you would expect the junction between two routes to be outside the town, but not here; they connected right on the market square.

For anyone looking for a busy urban scene to model, this is ideal.

This is a train on the Fleurville route with a Bicabine locomotive.

The St Trivier line used conventional locomotives.

Behind the trains is the tramways station, a grand affair right in the middle of town.

This was the station; not bad for two little metre gauge tramways! Most of the building was a goods shed, in fact.

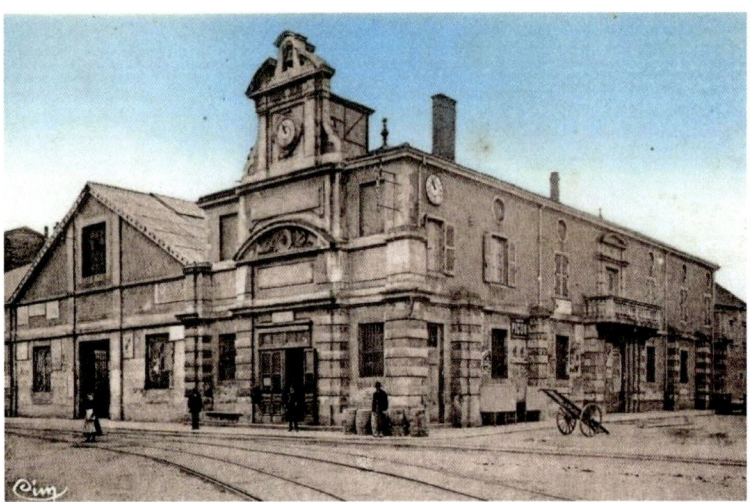

The old tramway station is now an arts centre.

SOCIÉTÉ DES CHEMINS DE FER ÉCONOMIQUES DU SUD-EST

(1re et 2e classes.)

TRÉVOUX A SAINT-TRIVIER-DE-COURTES

1re cl. De Trévoux	2e cl.	kil.	(77)	De Saint-Laurent-lès-Mâcon.	Mercredis et jours de grande foire à St-Laurent-lès-Mâcon.		Mercredis seulement.			Vers St-Laurent-lès-Mâcon.		
			●Trévoux ..... dép.	...	...	4 30	6 54	7 58	12 10	16 »	19 2	20 25
» 25	» 15	2	Pont-de-Trévoux(h)	—	—	4 33	6 57	8 2	12 13	16 3	19 4	20 28
» 35	» 20	4	St-Didier-St-Bern(h	...	...	4 42	7 6	8 11	12 22	16 12	19 13	20 37
» 50	» 30	6	Riottier (halte)	—	—	4 47	7 11	8 16	12 27	16 17	19 18	20 42
» 60	» 35	7	●Jassans (188)	...	4 5	5 1	7 16	8 35	12 43	16 35	19 23	20 47
» 75	» 45	9	Beauregard	—	4 10	5 6	—	8 42	12 49	16 41	—	—
» 90	» 55	11	Fareins	...	4 16	5 12	...	8 49	12 56	16 47	...	...
1 25	» 75	15	Messimy	—	4 27	5 23	...	9 1	13 8	16 58	...	...
1 30	» 80	16	Lurcy (halte)	...	4 32	5 28	...	9 7	13 14	17 3	...	...
1 55	1 »	19	Montmerle	—	4 43	5 40	...	9 23	13 30	17 14	...	...
1 80	1 15	22	Pont-de-Bellev. (h.)	...	4 52	5 49	...	9 32	13 39	17 23	...	...
1 90	1 20	24	Guéreins		4 57	5 54	...	9 35	13 45	17 28	...	...
2 05	1 30	25	Genouilleux		5 2	5 59	...	9 43	13 51	17 34	...	...
2 20	1 40	27	Mogneneins		5 11	6 8	...	9 55	14 3	17 47	...	...
2 55	1 60	31	Thoissey		5 32	6 25	...	10 10	14 21	18 4	...	...
2 70	1 70	33	St-Didier-sur-Chal.		5 42	6 37	...	10 21	14 31	18 13	...	...
2 95	1 85	36	Garnerans		5 53	6 48	...	10 35	14 42	18 24	...	...
3 30	2 05	40	Cormoranche		6 3	6 59	...	10 46	14 53	18 35	...	...
3 45	2 15	42	Grièges		6 10	7 6	...	10 52	15 »	18 41	...	...
3 70	2 30	45	Laiz		6 19	7 14	—	11 1	15 9	18 50	...	...
3 80	2 35	46	●Pont-de-Veyle (80)		6 28	7 25		11 12	15 18	19 1	...	...
4 05	2 50	49	Crottet		6 35	7 32		11 19	15 25	19 11	...	...
4 20	2 60	51	●La Madeleine.. arr.		6 41	7 38		11 25	15 31	19 17	...	...
			(185, 188) dép.	6 42	7 15	8 23		11 55	16 4		...	...
4 30	2 65	52	Replonges	6 48	7 22	8 31		12 2	16 11		...	...
4 55	2 80	55	Feillens	6 56	7 33	8 40		12 10	16 20		...	...
4 75	2 95	58	Manziat	7 5	7 45	8 52		12 21	16 32		...	...
5 »	3 10	61	Ozan	7 15	7 53	9 »		12 28	16 35		...	...
5 20	3 20	63	Boz	7 21	8 3	9 7	11 40	12 36	16 47		...	...
5 45	3 35	66	Gorrevod	7 39	8 10	9 16	11 49	12 44	16 56		...	...
5 45	3 35	66	●Pont-de-Vaux (171)	7 45	8 15	9 31	11 54	12 54	17 8		...	...
5 70	3 50	69	St-Bénigne	7 58	—	9 44	—	13 7	17 20		...	...
5 95	3 65	72	Chavannes-s-Reyss.	8 6	...	9 52	...	13 15	17 28		...	...
6 10	3 75	74	Vescours (halte) ...	8 14	—	9 59	—	13 21	17 34		...	...
6 40	3 95	78	●St-Trivier-d-C. (93)	8 25	...	10 10	...	13 32	17 45	—	...	...

AMBÉRIEU A CERDON

1re cl. D'Ambérieu	2e cl.	kil.	(83, 84, 68)			Dimanches et fêtes.			
			●Ambérieu-P.L.M. dép.	6 50	8 25		11 40	15 »	20 40
» 25	» 15	2	Ambérieu-Ville	6 55	8 30		11 45	15 5	20 45
» 35	» 20	4	Douvres-Chem.-N. h	7 »	8 37		11 50	15 10	20 50
» 50	» 30	6	Douvres-Coutel. h.	7 5	8 40		11 55	15 15	20 55
» 60	» 35	7	Ambronay	7 10	8 45		12 »	15 20	21 »
» 80	» 50	10	●St-Jean-le-V. (186	7 30	9 5		12 20	15 40	21 20
1 15	» 70	14	La Route (halte) ...	7 40	9 15		12 30	15 50	21 30
1 30	» 80	16	Neuville-sur-Ain ...	7 50	9 25		12 40	16 »	21 40
1 55	1 »	19	Poncin	7 56	9 31		12 46	16 6	21 46
1 65	1 05	20	Leymiat	8 2	9 38		12 52	16 12	21 52
1 80	1 15	22	Préau-Mérignat (h)	8 5	9 42		12 57	16 16	21 56
1 90	1 20	23	Cerdon .... arr.	8 10	9 46		13 »	16 20	22 »

VIRIEU-LE-GRAND A RUFFIEU

1re cl. De Virieu	2e cl.	kil.	(101)				Excepté les samedis et veilles de fêtes lég.	Samedis et veilles de fêtes légales.
			●Virieu-le-Gr.. dép.	9 30	12 55	17 5	20 26	21 35
» 35	» 20	4	●Artemare (80)	9 55	13 10	17 20	20 40	21 48
» 50	» 30	6	Artemare-Ville	10 2	13 18	17 28	20 45	21 58
» 75	» 45	9	Don	10 12	13 28	17 38	20 54	22 8
1 »	» 60	12	Vieu	10 22	13 39	17 49	21 4	22 18
1 15	» 70	15	Champagne-Luthe.	10 28	13 46	17 57	21 12	22 24
1 30	» 80	16	Fitignieu	10 38	13 56	18 7	21 22	22 33
1 50	» 95	18	Sutrieu	10 48	14 5	18 15	21 31	22 40
1 65	1 05	20	Lompnieu	10 55	14 14	18 22	21 38	22 45
1 90	1 20	23	Ruffieu .... arr.	11 8	14 27	18 35	21 50	22 57

PONT-D'AIN A JUJURIEUX

1re cl. De Pont d'Ain	2e cl.	kil.	(80, 68)			Dim. et fêtes							
			●Pont-d'Ain dép.	...	6 25		11 10	...	...	15 5	...	19 »	...
» 40	» 25	5	Hauterive	5 19	6 38		11 24	—	—	15 18	—	19 12	—
» 50	» 30	6	●St-Jean-le-Vieux	5 25	7 25	9 15	11 33	12 25	13 10	15 41	17 50	19 25	21 15
» 65	» 40	8	Riez (halte)	5 32	7 32	9 30	11 40	12 32	13 17	15 48	17 57	19 [illegible]	21 22
» 75	» 45	9	Jujurieux ..... arr.	5 35	7 45	9 35	11 43	12 35	13 20	15 51	18 »	19 35	21 25

SAINT-TRIVIER-DE-COURTES A TRÉVOUX

1re cl. De St-Trivier	2e cl.	kil.				De Saint-Laurent-lès-Mâcon.			Mercredis seulement.		Mercredis et jours de grande foire à St-Laurent-lès-Mâcon.		Vers St-Laurent-lès-Mâcon.
			●St-Trivier-d-C. dép.	...	...		6 12	9 15	...	...	...	14 20	17 8
» 40	» 25	5	Vescours (halte) ...	—	—		6 23	9 27	...	...	—	14 31	17 19
» 60	» 35	7	Chavannes-sur-Rey	...	...		6 29	9 35	—	—	...	14 38	17 29
» 80	» 50	10	St-Bénigne	—	—		6 37	9 44	...	...	—	14 46	17 38
1 »	» 60	12	●Pont-de-Vaux	...	...		6 52	10 »	11 20	...	14 20	15 5	17 59
1 05	» 65	13	Gorrevod	—	—		6 57	10 6	11 25	—	14 30	15 10	18 5
1 25	» 75	15	Boz	..	...		7 8	10 15	11 35	...	14 39	15 19	18 14
1 50	» 95	18	Ozan	—	—		7 15	10 22		—	14 45	15 27	18 21
1 65	1 05	20	Manziat	...	...		7 22	10 30		...	14 54	15 35	18 30
2 »	1 25	24	Feillens	—	—		7 34	10 43		—	15 10	15 48	18 45
2 20	1 40	27	Replonges	...	...		7 41	10 50		...	15 17	15 54	18 51
2 30	1 45	28	●La Madeleine. arr.	—	—		7 47	10 56		—	15 23	16 »	18 58
			dép.	...	...	4 43	8 28	12 32		...	16 4	16 50	
2 45	1 55	30	Crottet	—	—	4 49	8 34	12 39		—	16 10	16 57	
2 65	1 65	32	●Pont-de-Veyle	...	...	4 57	8 43	12 56	—	...	16 20	17 10	
2 80	1 75	34	Laiz	—	—	5 5	8 54	13 3	...	—	16 28	17 18	
3 05	1 90	37	Grièges	...	...	5 14	9 »	13 12	—	...	16 37	17 27	
3 20	2 »	39	Cormoranche	—	—	5 20	9 6	13 19	...	—	16 45	17 33	
3 45	2 15	42	Garnerans	...	...	5 31	9 16	13 30	—	...	16 56	17 44	
3 80	2 35	46	St-Didier-sur-Chal .	—	—	5 43	9 29	13 42	...	—	17 10	17 57	
3 95	2 45	48	Thoissey	...	...	5 56	9 44	13 55	—	...	17 30	18 20	
4 20	2 60	51	Mogneneins	—	—	6 7	9 57	14 6	...	—	17 43	18 32	
4 45	2 75	54	Genouilleux	...	...	6 15	10 5	14 14	—	...	17 50	18 41	
4 60	2 85	56	Guéreins	—	—	6 20	10 11	14 19	...	—	17 56	18 47	
4 70	2 90	57	Pont-de-Bellev. (h.)	...	...	6 25	10 16	14 24	—	...	18 1	18 52	
4 85	3 »	59	Montmerle	—	—	6 30	10 22	14 33	...	—	18 12	19 5	—
5 10	3 15	62	Lurcy (halte)	...	...	6 45	10 39	14 43	—	...	18 22	19 15	...
5 25	3 25	64	Messimy	—	—	6 50	10 45	14 48	...	—	18 27	19 21	—
5 60	3 45	68	Fareins	...	...	7 1	10 57	15 »	—	...	18 38	19 33	...
5 70	3 50	69	Beauregard	—	—	7 7	11 4	15 7	...	—	18 45	19 40	—
5 95	3 65	72	●Jassans	4 »	6 15	7 21	11 20	15 20	...	18 30	18 50	19 55	...
6 »	3 70	73	Riottier (halte)	4 5	6 20	7 26	11 25	15 25	—	18 35	—	20 »	—
6 20	3 80	75	St-Didier-St-Bern(h	4 10	6 25	7 31	11 31	15 30	...	18 40	..	20 5	...
6 35	3 90	77	Pt-de-Trévoux (h.).	4 19	6 34	7 40	11 40	15 39	—	18 49	—	20 14	—
6 60	3 95	78	●Trévoux ..... arr.	4 23	6 37	7 43	11 45	15 45	...	18 53	...	20 18	...

CERDON A AMBÉRIEU

1re cl. De Cerdon	2e cl.	kil.			Dimanches et fêtes.		Dim. et fêtes.		
			Cerdon .... dép.	5 10		9 30	10 45	13 25	17 5
» 25	» 15	2	Préau-Mérignat (h.)	5 13		9 33	10 50	13 28	17 10
» 25	» 15	3	Leymiat	5 18		9 38	10 54	13 32	17 15
» 40	» 25	5	Poncin	5 24		9 41	11 1	13 38	17 19
» 60	» 35	7	Neuville-sur-Ain ...	5 30		9 50	11 6	13 43	17 23
» 80	» 50	10	La Route (halte) ...	5 40		10 »	11 16	13 53	17 35
1 05	» 65	13	●St-Jean-le-Vieux ..	6 »	7 30	10 32	11 26	14 15	17 56
1 40	» 90	17	Ambronay	6 10	7 40	10 42		14 25	18 5
1 50	» 95	18	Douvres-Coutel.(h.)	6 15	7 45	10 47		14 30	18 10
1 65	1 05	20	Douvres-Ch-Neuf(h	6 20	7 50	10 52		14 35	18 15
1 80	1 15	22	Ambérieu-Ville	6 25	7 55	10 57		14 40	18 20
1 90	1 20	23	●Ambérieu-P.L.M. arr.	6 30	8 »	11 2		14 45	18 25

RUFFIEU A VIRIEU-LE-GRAND

1re cl. De Ruffieu	2e cl.	kil.					
			Ruffieu .... dép.	6 5	10 25	14 30	18 36
» 35	» 20	4	Lompnieu	6 18	10 38	14 42	18 47
» 40	» 25	5	Sutrieu	6 25	10 46	14 49	18 53
» 65	» 40	8	Fitignieu	6 34	10 56	14 59	19 2
» 80	» 50	10	Champagne-Luthé.	6 43	11 5	15 8	19 10
1 »	» 60	12	Vieu	6 50	11 12	15 15	19 16
1 25	» 75	15	Don	7 »	11 21	15 25	19 25
1 40	» 90	17	Artemare-Ville	7 10	11 30	15 35	19 34
1 55	1 »	19	●Artemare P.L.M. ..	7 20	11 40	15 45	19 43
1 90	1 20	23	●Virieu-le-Gr. arr.	7 35	11 53	16 »	19 54

JUJURIEUX A PONT-D'AIN

1re c. De Jujur.	2e c.	k.					Dim. et fêtes.							
			Jujurieux .. dép.	...	5 33	8 45	10 15	12 5	12 45	14 »	17 30	18 5	19 45	21 35
» 25	» 15	1	Riez (halte)	—	5 42	8 48	10 18	12 8	12 48	14 3	17 33	18 8	19 48	21 38
» 25	» 15	3	●St-Jean-le-Vieux	5 10	5 53	8 55	10 30	12 15	12 55	14 30	17 40	18 17	19 55	21 45
» 40	» 25	5	Hauterive	5 15	5 58	—	10 35	—	—	14 35	—	18 22	—	—
» 75	» 45	9	●Pont-d'Ain arr.	—	6 13	...	10 50	...	...	14 50	...	18 37	...	...

CHAPTER 5
PONT de VAUX PART 2

So what of the bridge in the name of Pont de Vaux? The wide River Saone ran past the town, across the route of the tramway to Fleurville. Don't get carried away with thoughts of the tramway company building a bridge across the river though – new bridges cost money. No, they simply laid their tracks along the side of the road out of town and when they came to the existing road bridge over the tracks went, despite the pronounced hump in the middle of the bridge. The line then crossed the adjacent canal as well, and it all makes a very appealing scene well worth considering by the modeller.

This is the canal bridge, a metal bow string girder.

What a delightful scene!

CHAPTER 6

CHATEAUNEUF EN THYMERAIS PART 1

This was the line that didn't know when to stop extending!

Chateauneuf en Thymerais is a small town, in fact a very small town….in 1901 the population was only 1326 people. Despite this though it had three stations in the space of thirty years, plus another short branch line!

The tramway to Châteauneuf-en-Thymerais was part of the Eure et Loire network. In 1894 the General Council of Eure et Loir launched a study into building a tram network, with the declaration of public interest on 27/02/1897 which authorized the construction of the network. The tramway from Saint-Sauveur to Châteauneuf opened on 01.22.1899.

The original station was on the edge of town, a lovely little terminus that would be perfect for a model in a limited space….this is the inspirational bit!

It had a tiny brick station building, a goods shed, loco shed, water tank, all the essential ingredients in a tiny space., perfect for a narrow gauge layout.

The original station with the town beyond, following the opening of the extension into the town centre..

The station building is on the right, the goods shed behind it served from a turntable, and the loco shed is to the left of the station building.

The shelter was small but beautifully decorated with red and yellow brick.

This is the view from the road from the town; all three buildings can be seen.

The shelter with the goods shed behind it. On the left is the water tank.

At other stations on the E&L system with similar architecture there was a house/station building standing back from the line and there may well have been a similar structure at Chateauneuf which doesn't show in the pictures.

Remarkably, the goods shed and the loco shed survive in good condition.

The little station did not remain a terminus for long; it was too far out of town to be convenient for passengers. The line was extended into the town proper, so it could also form the basis for a through station on a layout.

CHAPTER 7

CHATEAUNEUF EN THYMERAIS PART 2

By the early 1900's the trains were running beyond the little terminus into the town to a new station on the Rue Jean Jaures where the road was wide enough to squeeze in a station. This was pretty much purely for passengers, all large goods traffic continued to use the original station and the loco shed there remained in use too.

So far, very sensible – the town now had a conveniently placed station, the line running to it along streets past the Mairie in the town centre. However, another part of town still felt left out, so a short branch was built to the Place St Clair from a junction right on the crossroads in the middle of town where it terminated in a simple loop. Trains now ran along here, reversed, and ran back to continue their journey….all for a population of 1326 people!

So it remained…for now.

This is the station on Rue Jean Jaures, a typical French station building. There is a small attached goods shed for small items such as parcels. The town centre is in the distance by the tower.

The toilet facilities might have been OK in a rural location, but this was in the middle of town!

The station is seen on the left. This is the Place St Clair...the tramway is on the right in front of the buildings.

The line to Place St Clair is running towards the camera. The line to Rue Jean Jaures ran through a narrow gap on the left. between two buildings, opened out in 1928 when the road was widened.

This little station served the town perfectly well until 1928, when someone got big ideas.

A new metre gauge line was proposed, an electric trolley line this time, to St Sauveur, another small town. This was in 1928, when narrow gauge railways all over France were in financial trouble, but not only was it proposed, it was actually built!

In Chateauneuf the line to Place St Clair was closed. A new halt was built right in the town centre by the crossroads, and now the line carried straight on along Rue Jean Jaures and on out of town towards St Saveur. The Rue Jean Jaures was widened to form a proper crossroads in the middle of the town where the new halt was. Trains had always picked up passengers there, but now it was officially a stopping place.

The new line opened in 1928 for freight, but there is some uncertainty as to whether it was ever electrified. It ran a passenger service in 1931 – just in 1931! – using a Renault RS petrol railcar. Incredibly, in the same year it was extended to La Loupe.

In 1932, all the metre gauge lines of the E&L were closed, except the one to Chateauneuf. That continued to operate until 1936 using a railcar, probably the same Renault.

The new line hung on until 1933 carrying some freight, and then it quietly closed. The rails were lifted in 1937.

This is the end of the Rue Jean Jaures in about 1935, with the line of the new tramway crossing the road, overgrown and disused from the look of it. The picture seems to confirm that it was never electrified. This is the only picture I have ever seen of the new line.

The Rue Jean Jaures was converted into a dual carriageway in the late 1930's; the distinctive house marks the site of the station, and it is still there today.

I realise this isn't really inspirational, unless it inspires someone to recognise a lost cause when they see it!

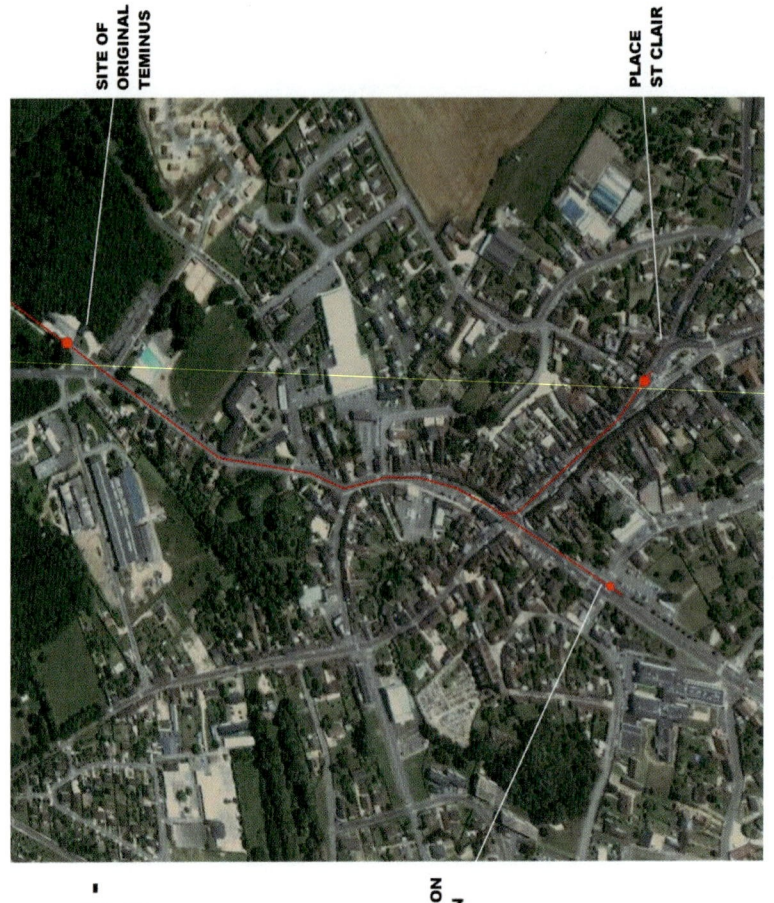

SITE OF ORIGINAL TEMINUS

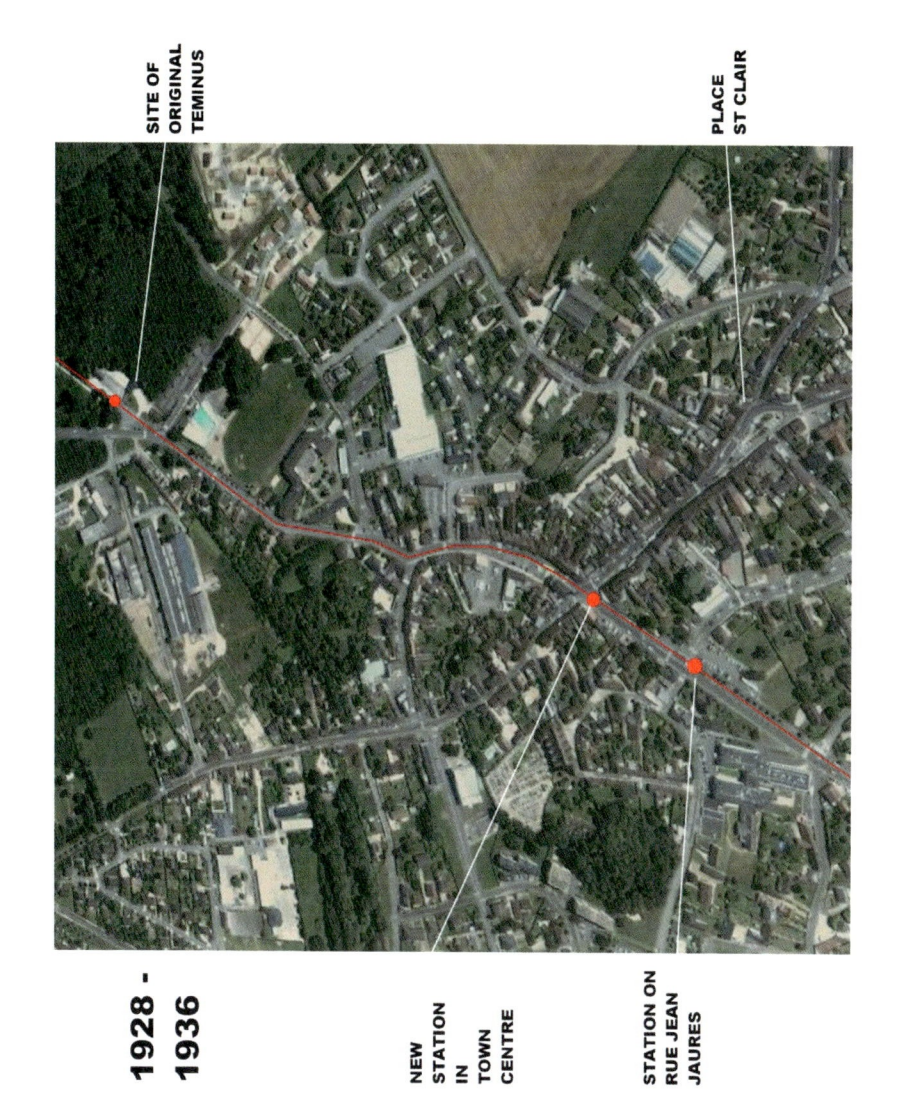

PLACE ST CLAIR

1928 - 1936

NEW STATION IN TOWN CENTRE

STATION ON RUE JEAN JAURES

CHAPTER 8

BREZOLLES

Staying with the E&L system here's another little terminus that later became a through station, Brezolles.

A line opened from Dreux to Brezolles on January 8th 1899, to this little station:

![Brezolles - La Gare du Tramway postcard]

The train is approaching from Dreux, past the loco shed. On the right is the small station building and behind that is the goods shed reached via a turntable. On the right is a wagon weighbridge. That's the whole station in the picture; just four points and a wagon turntable! The similarity to the original station at Chateauneuf is obvious. The building to the right of the loco shed was not part of the station.

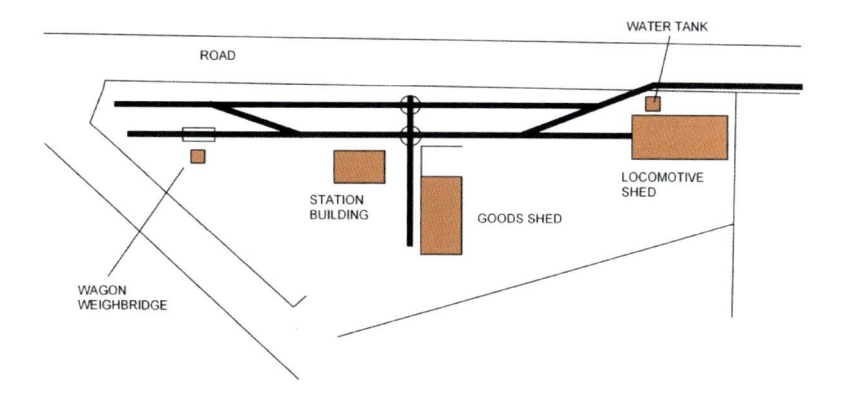

It remained as built until 1905 when work began on extending the line to Senoches. This section opened on August 15th 1907, and was to prove the least profitable on the whole E&L system.

As far as Brezolles was concerned the station was expanded and gained a more substantial station building though much of the charm was gone.

By 1930 the passenger trains were being run by autorails as well as steam in an effort to cut costs but it didn't work. Goods receipts fell by 30% in 1933; it couldn't last. Both lines from Brezolles closed on May 26th that year.

Pictures of the station are rare, understandably with the early closure, but it is the little terminus that is likely to appeal to modellers.

Finally, a more cheerful picture of celebrating crowds on the opening of the extension in 1907…presumably none of them had invested any money in it!

CHAPTER 9

ST JAMES – AVERANCHES

Here is another little known yet delightfully appealing station, at the end of a metre gauge tramway that ran from a terminus in Avranches for 17km to the town of St James.

Built by the Tramways Normand the line was opened in 1901 and only lasted until 1933. There were stations at Pontaubault and Juilley as well as numerous halts.

This is the tramway station in Avranches which between 1907 and 1914 was shared by the electric tramcars of the town tramway.

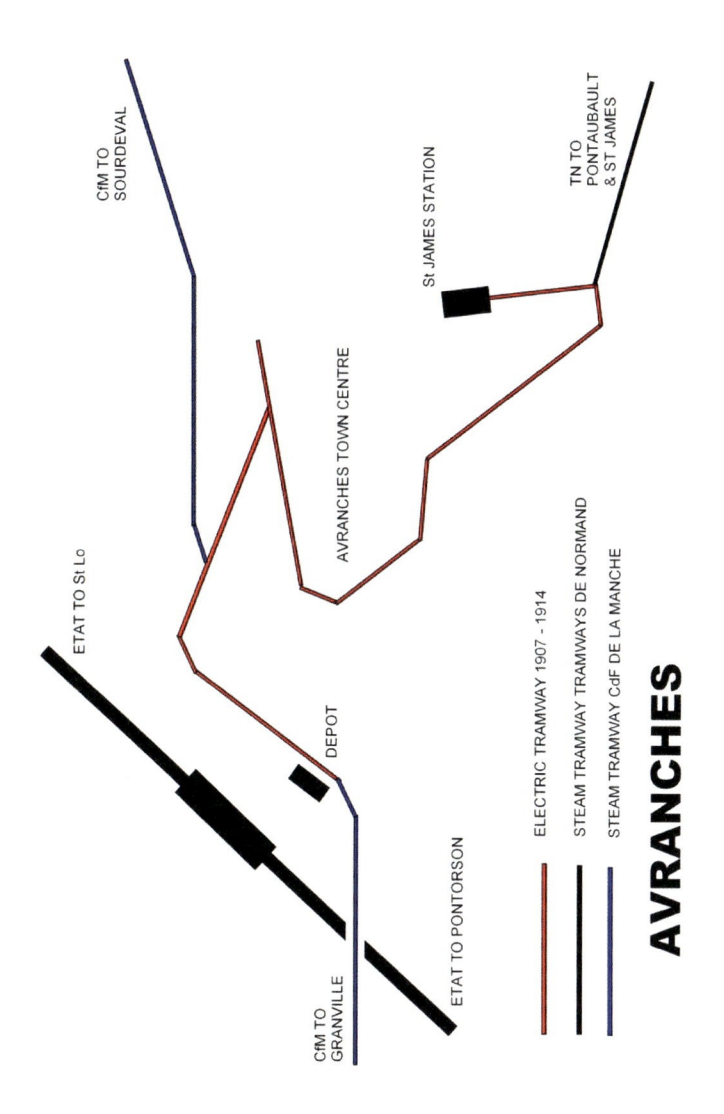

After the electric tramway closed in 1914 the St James line was physically separated from the other meter gauge in the city, the CdF de la Manche to Granville and Sourdeval.

59 AVRANCHES. — Le Boulevard de l'Est et le Tramway de Saint-James

Meilleures amitiés.
H. Lodemé

73 AVRANCHES. — Le Boulevard de l'Est et le Tramway de Saint-James. — LL.

Page 41

The line crossed the existing road bridge at Pontaubault.

The loco's look like Corpet Louvet 030 tanks.

The little terminus was another gem, ideal as the basis for a model.

It had a station building with a separate goods shed, and a single tracked loco shed at the end of the line.

It's a simple little terminus, with three loops and a siding off to the loco shed…. typically French narrow gauge and small enough to model in a reasonable space.

CHAPTER 10
TIGY TO CHATEAUNEUF-SUR-LOIRE

Next, a whole branch line to inspire you; metre gauge again of course, and this time built by the Tramways de Sologne and opened in 1905. It was another early closure, in 1934.

It ran from the main line of the system at Tigy for 7km to the main line station at Chateauneuf-sur-Loire.

First, as a taster, here is what the traveller leaving the train at Chateauneuf-sur-Loire would have seen……

(I know it's not narrow gauge but I couldn't resist it!)

The curious traveller might have lingered to watch this….

..or this…

However, pity the poor traveller to Tigy, because they had to walk out of the main line station, and then things became rather less salubrious!

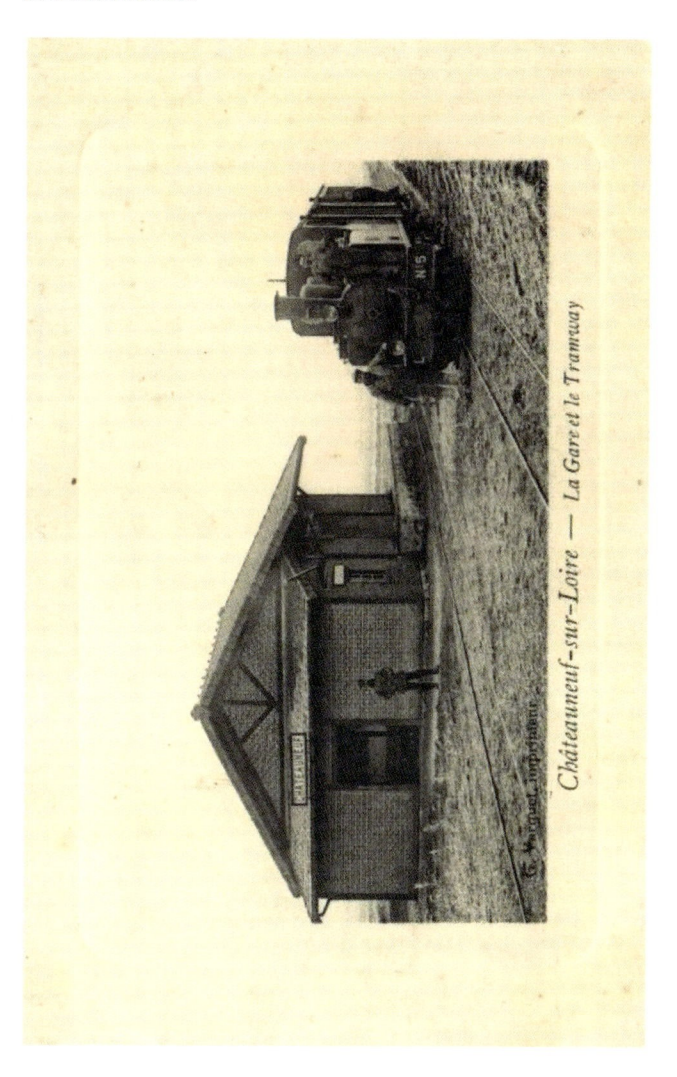

Châteauneuf-sur-Loire — La Gare et le Tramway

Nevertheless, it was transport at least, and eventually it would set off across the fields, not rushing, but making progress all the same...in places even rising above the fields on this structure, part of which still exists...

After a mere 7km, Tigy would be reached, that delightfully named town with an equally delightful little junction station.

500 — Tigy - La Gare

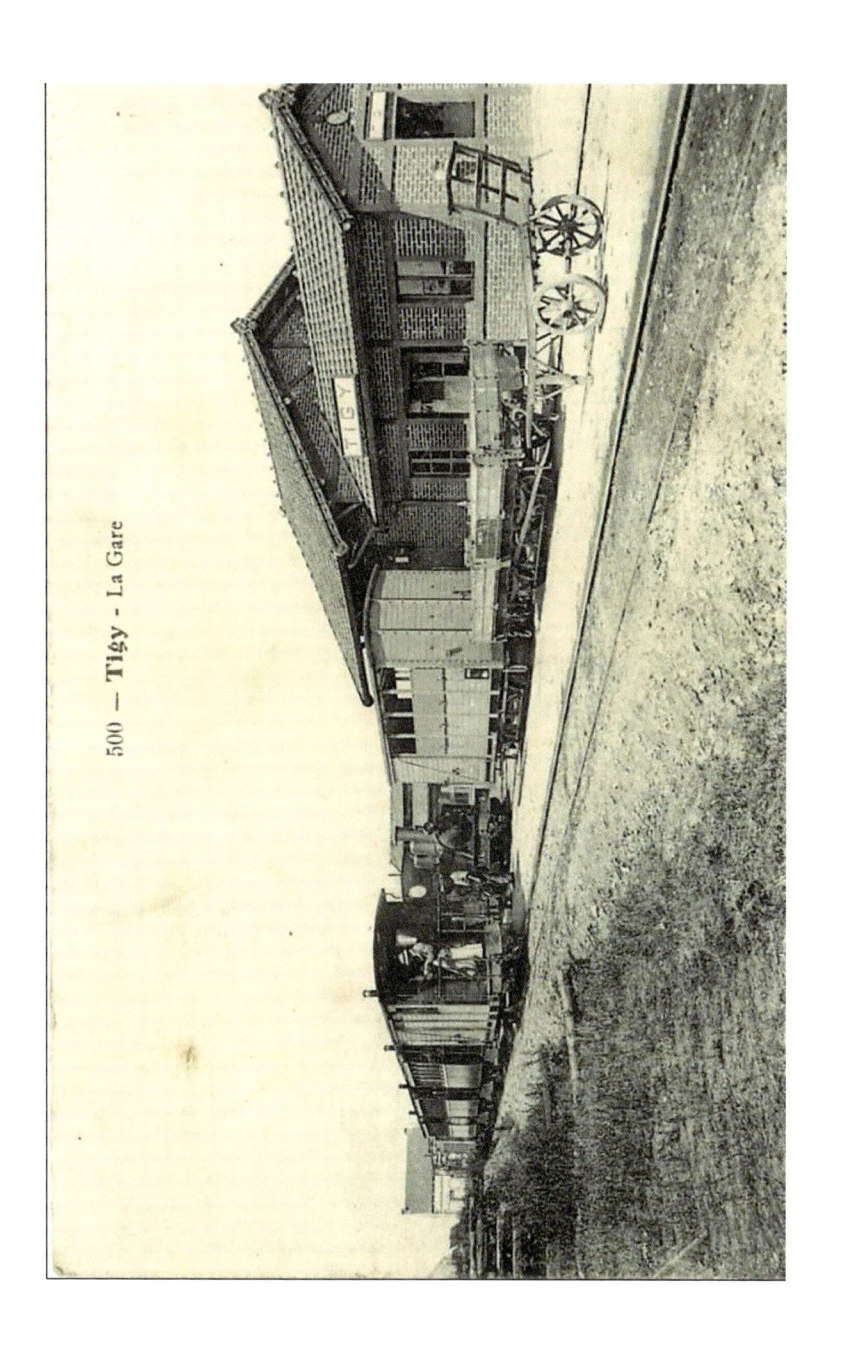

TIGY (Loiret). - La Gare

6 – **Tigy** (Loiret) – La Gare du Tramway

CHAPTER 11
CdF DE LA VALLEE DE CELLES

This little line I have included because of the distinctive and attractive architecture, quite unlike the usual narrow gauge French stations. It ran along the Celles valley in the Vosages department which apart from forestry, sawmills and agriculture also housed a large textile works.

The opening as far as Allarmont was on June 24, 1907 , then the rest of the line on July 26 for passengers and 1st August for goods. It ran between Celles sur Plaine, Allarmont, Vexaincourt, Luvigny and Raon sur Plaine.

This is the opening day train, suitably decorated.

The line was closed for a period during both world wars – it was in just the wrong place! When traffic resumed in 1946 the line was cut back at the Raon end and the service reduced to one train a day – nor surprisingly it closed in 1950, the victim as usual of road competition.

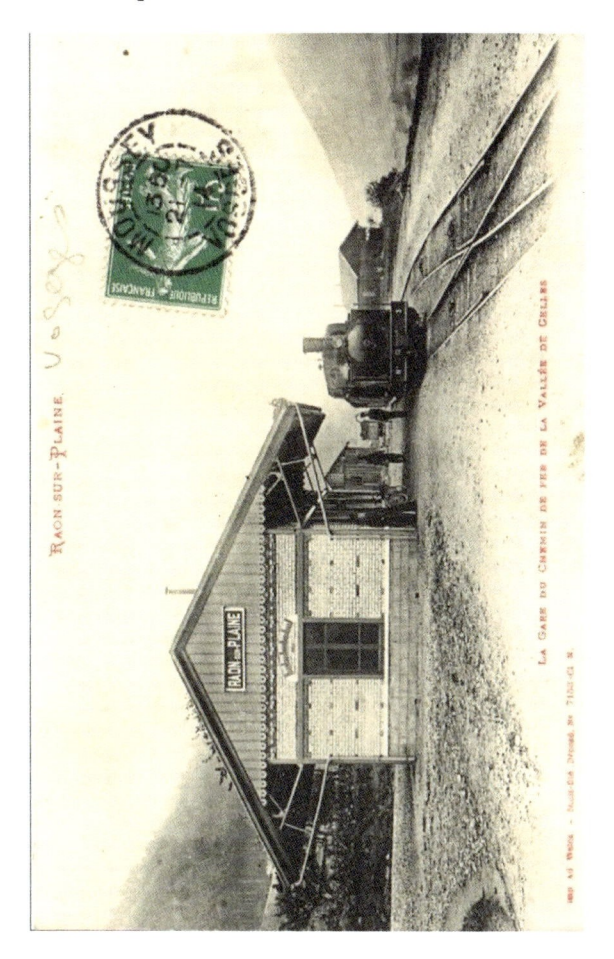

This is the reason for including the line here – these lovely and unusual station buildings. They were built at all the stations; this one is at Raon, the terminus.

The pit seems to be in an odd place. The tiny building to the left seems to be the toilet facilities!

This view shows the goods shed and loco shed as well.

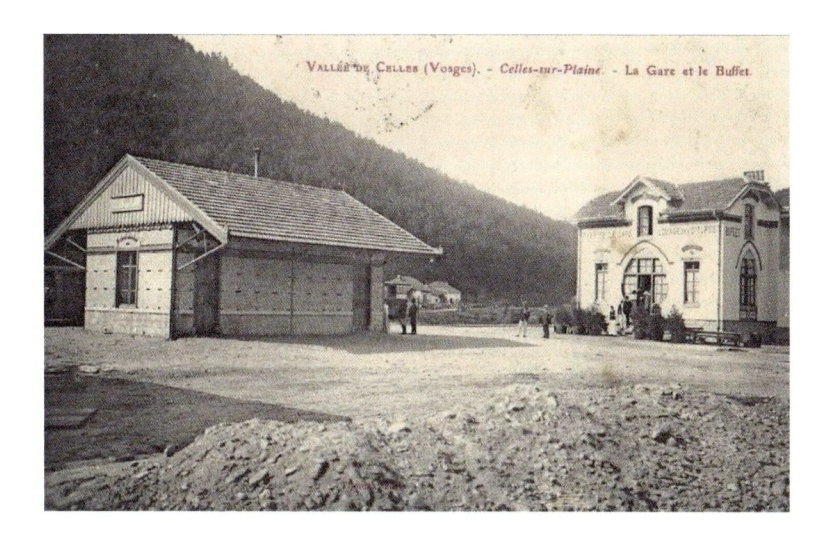

This is the other terminus, Celles sur Plaine, with the buffet beyond the station building. We'll come back to that in a minute.

The stations were built in yellow brick with red brick trim on a stone foundation, and a tiled roof. They are just the right size for a small layout.

That Buffet…wouldn't it make a nice model too?

When it opened in 1907 it looked like this, just the right size to add to a layout.

But then it began to grow!

A Hotel was added, and at least they matched the existing architecture. By the time the line closed it was even bigger…

Two more pictures….

The line was very typical in its loco's and stock, but at some point early on this little railcar was tried. It doesn't seem to have lasted long.

CHEMIN DE FER DE LA VALLÉE DE CELLES

RAON-EST A RAON-SUR-PLAINE

ALLER

De Raon		ALLER	1.2cl.	1.2cl.	1re2cl	1re2cl Dim. etFêtes	1re2cl Se- maine	1re2cl Dim. etFêtes	1re2cl Du 1er Juillet au 15 sept.	1re2cl Se- maine	1re2cl Dim. etFêtes	1re2cl	1re2cl Sauf les samedis, dimanches, Veilles et jours de fêtes.	1re2cl Samedis, dimanches, Veilles et jours de fêtes.
fr.c.	k.													
» 15	0	●Raon-Est(92) dép.	6 30	8 15	10 10	11 15	11 15	13 15	15 15	14 55	15 20	17 2	20 20	20 25
» 30	1	Raon-l'Étape... { dép.	6 38	8 23	10 20	11 23	11 23	13 23	15 20		15 26	17 10	20 26	20 33
» 30	4	{ arr.	6 40	8 30				13 35	15 27					20 35
» 70	8	La Trouche (halte).	6 48	8 39	11 30	11 30	11 35	13 44	15 35	15 9	15 32	20 10	20 32	20 44
1 15	11	Scierie Lajus (halte)	7 1	8 51	11 38	11 38	11 44	13 57	15 48	15 18	15 41	20 19	20 41	20 56
1 25	12	Celles-sur-Plaine...	7 11	9 11	11 51	11 51	11 56	14 12	16 1	15 26	15 47	20 31	20 43	5
1 55	15	Sortie de Celles (arrt	7 13	9 13	12 4	12 6	12 30	14 22	16 3	15 36	15 57		20 53	17
1 85	17	Route de Badonv.(h	7 23	9 23	12 16	12 16	12 42	14 28	16 13	15 57	16 2		20 59	23
2 05	20	Allarmont...	7 30	9 30	12 22	12 22	12 48	14 35	16 19	16 5	16 10		21 8	32
2 35	22	Vexaincourt...	7 38	9 38	12 31	12 31	12 57	14 37	16 28	16 16	16 19		21 14	38
2 60	24	Luvigny...	7 44	9 44	12 37	12 37	13 4	14 43	16 34	16 32	16 32		21 26	44
		●Raon-s-Plainearr.	7 50	9 50	12 43	12 43	13 10	14 49	16 40	16 42	16 42		21 20	

RETOUR

		RETOUR	1re2cl	1re2cl	1re2cl	1re2cl Se- maine	1re2cl Dim. etFêtes	1re2cl Dim. et Fêtes du 1er Juill. au 15 sept.	1re2cl	1re2cl Se- maine	1re2cl Dim. etFêtes	1re2cl
		Raon-s-Plaine dép.	...	6 30	8 30	10 30	10 35	13 30	...	14 55	15 20	18 20
		Luvigny...	...	6 36	8 36	10 36	10 41	13 36	...	15 9	15 26	18 26
		Vexaincourt...	...	6 42	8 42	10 42	10 47	13 42	...	15 15	15 32	18 32
		Allarmont...	...	6 51	8 51	10 51	10 56	13 51	...	15 18	15 41	18 41
		Route de Badonv.(h	...	6 57	8 57	10 57	11 2	13 57	...	15 26	15 47	18 47
		Sortie de Celles (arrt	...	7 7	9 7	11 7	11 12	14 7	...	15 36	15 57	2 57
		Celles-sur-Plaine...	...	7 11	9 11	11 22	11 18	14 13	...	16 5	16 2	19 5
		Scierie Lajus (halte	...	7 19	9 18	11 30	11 26	14 21	...	16 18	16 10	19 13
		La Trouche (halte).	...	7 31	9 32	11 44	11 38	14 33	12 50	16 32	16 22	19 26
		Raon-l'Étape...	6 »	7 43	9 42	11 58	11 50	14 45	»	16 42	16 32	19 40
		●Raon-Est.... arr.	6 10	7 53	9 52	12 8	12 »	14 55	» 13		16 42	19 50

CHAPTER 12

THE ST ROMAIN DE COLBOSC TRAMWAY

The St Romain de Colbosc tramway ran from 1896 to 1929, a proper urban street tramway, steam powered and full of character, a nice place to finish our tour of the lesser known French railways. It was metre gauge again, of course, and connected the middle of the town with the nearest station, Etainhus on the Paris to Le Harve line, 4km away. We are in the Seinne department this time.

When it opened it used a self-propelled steam railcar but that was soon replaced with something more reliable, conventional steam loco's. The line carried 100,000 people a year before the First World War, but nevertheless financially it was still pretty precarious. Traffic dropped through the 1920's until the inevitable closure.

As a prototype for a model it has a lot to offer, a proper urban tramway with proper steam loco's. The line looped around the town square, so an out and back layout would work well.

1656. ETAINHUS (Seine-Inf.) — La Gare et l'Hôtel

This is the mainline station to which the tramway ran, at Etainhus.

The tramway had no covered accommodation here, just the end of track and a run round loop. The main line station building was close by, as was the inevitable café.

7321. SAINT-ROMAIN-de-COLBOSC (Seine-Inf.) — Le Tramway au Dépôt

This is the tramway depot with a train passing – the loco is a standard Corpet Louvet tank but the American looking spark arresting chimney totally alters its appearance.

The following pictures show the urban area, with real street running, corners rather than bends and very tight clearances!

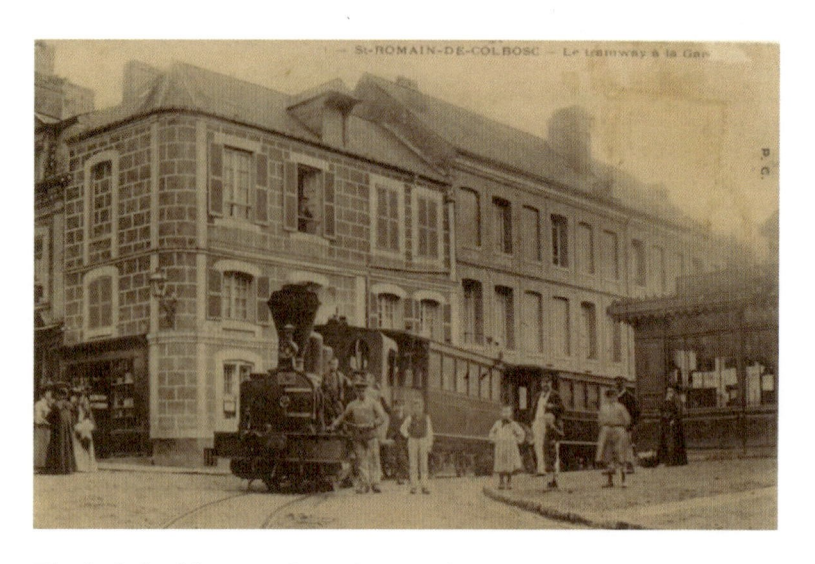

The little building on the right was the tramway station in the town centre.

(4) SAINT-ROMAIN DE-COLBOSC — L'Église

A Corpet Louvet that looks as though it belongs in the Wild West!

That curve could have come straight off a model too – the flanges must have squealed going round there.

In the middle of town, the tramway simply ran right round the church in a loop and then headed back to the main line station again.

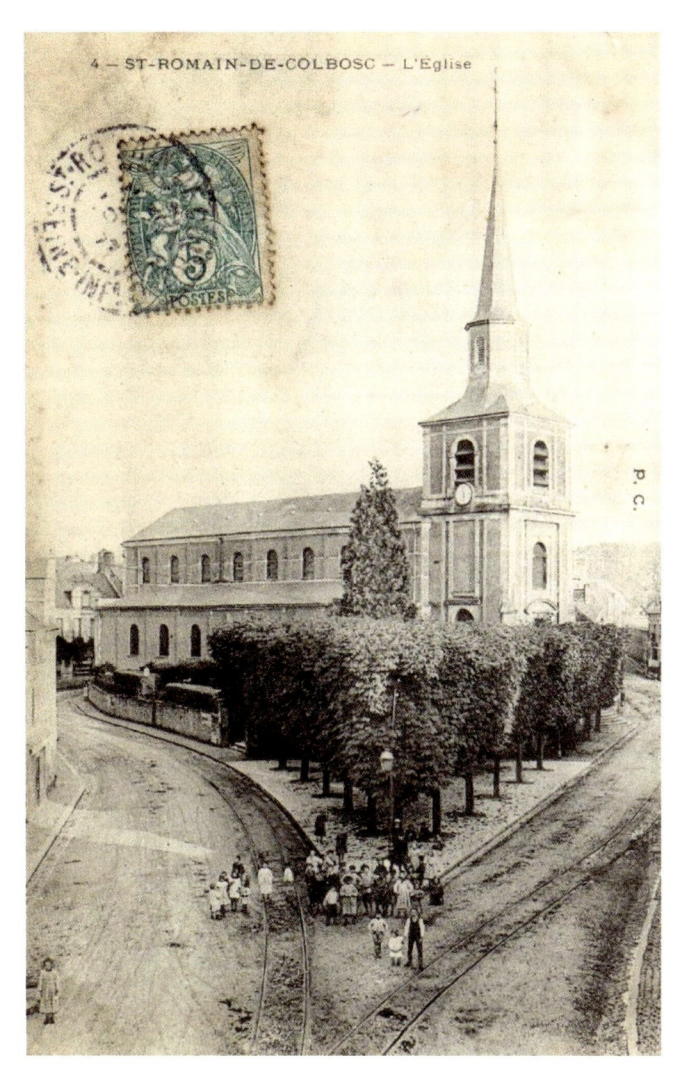

Saint-Romain-de-Colbosc. — L'Eglise

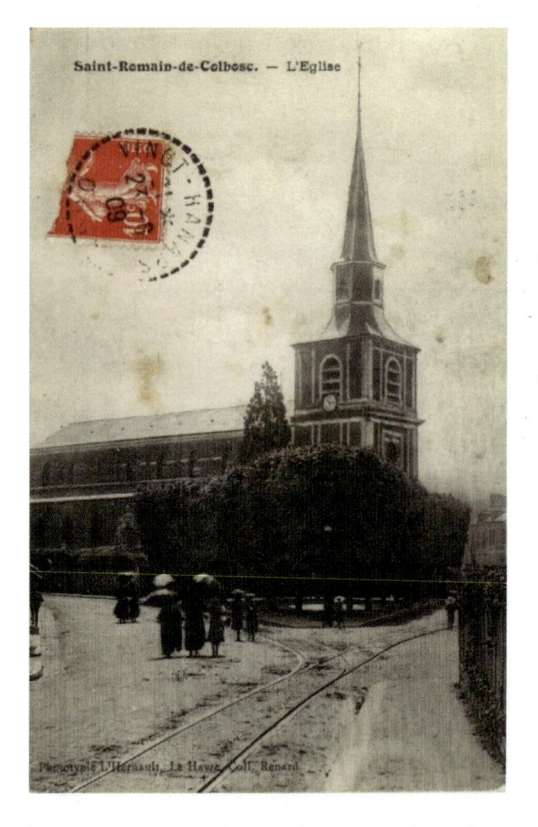

This more recent shot makes the route clear -

It amazes me to see how narrow the road was and that they were able to squeeze a tramway into such a confined space….exactly like we have to do with our models.

Well, there we are…my selection of inspirational French narrow gauge prototypes. The intention has not been to give a full history of any of these locations, but hopefully it will make you want to find out more. There should be enough variation across the twelve chapters for something to appeal to narrow gauge modellers.

My only problem is deciding which one to model ….I'd like to think I may have given some of you the same problem!

You might also enjoy these other books

THE THONES-ANNECY TRAMWAY.

THE THIZY TRAMWAY

NARROW GAUGE ON THE ILE DE RE AND THE ILE D'OLERON

Printed in Great Britain
by Amazon.co.uk, Ltd.,
Marston Gate.